THE
MOUNTAIN MAN
AND THE
PRESIDENT

BY DAVID WEITZMAN

Alex Haley, General Editor

ILLUSTRATIONS BY
CHARLES SHAW

STECK-VAUGHN
ELEMENTARY · SECONDARY · ADULT · LIBRARY

A Harcourt Company

For Arin, Brooks, and Peter

Published by Steck-Vaughn Company.

Text, illustrations, and cover art copyright © 1993 by Dialogue Systems, Inc., 627 Broadway, New York, New York 10012.

Cover art by Charles Shaw

Printed in China

13 14 15 16 1666 14 13

Library of Congress Cataloging-in-Publication Data

Weitzman, David L.
    The mountain man and the president / author, David
Weitzman; illustrator, Charles Shaw
        p.   cm.—(Stories of America)
    Summary: Discusses how the friendship between naturalist
John Muir and President Theodore Roosevelt brought about gov-
ernment protection of America's wilderness.
        ISBN 0-8114-7224-8 (hardcover)— ISBN 0-8114-8064-X (soft-
cover)
    1. Muir, John, 1838-1914—Juvenile literature. 2. Naturalists—
United States—Biography—Juvenile literature. 3. Roosevelt,
Theodore, 1858-1919—Juvenile literature. 4. Presidents—United
States—Biography—Juvenile literature. 5. Conservationists—
United States—Biography—Juvenile literature. [1. Muir, John,
1838-1914. 2. Naturalists. 3. Roosevelt, Theodore, 1858-1919.
4. Presidents. 5. Conservationists. 6. Conservation of natural
resources—History.] I. Shaw, Charles, 1941– ill. II. Title.
III. Series.
QH31.M78W45   1993
333.7'2'092273—dc20   92-23040
                                                               CIP
                                                                AC

ISBN-13: 978-0-8114-8064-2
4500428681   D E F G

Introduction
by Alex Haley, General Editor

We all have our own special places. I prefer the Tennessee hills and the forests of the Pacific Northwest. When I'm working on a book, I like to get away to sea and write. There is the quiet beauty, the majesty of nature to find peace and inspiration in. A writer needs that, people need that.

David Weitzman's book is about our need for special places. It's about the importance of the wilderness in our lives.

And even though it is set in the recent past, the early 1900s, it is also about the future. Our world has a few million, maybe a few billion, years of life in it. Our children—your children—and all the children to come will need the wilderness—for what it does for the soul and for what it does for life on our planet.

Contents

△△△ 1 △△△

To Any Place That Is Wild

On the western slope of California's Sierra Nevada mountains, there is a valley called Yosemite. Seven miles long and, in places, a mile wide, the valley was gouged out of the granite rocks by glaciers a million years ago. A river meanders along the valley floor. Here it flows in quiet pools and there it splashes with a deafening roar over great boulders.

In the spring and summer, the meadows along the river shimmer with red and yellow and pink and purple wildflowers. Among them graze families of deer, great bucks with velvet-covered antlers and does with their new spotted fawns. There are mountain lions, black bears, and a tiny little creature called a pika, whose loud, piercing whistle scares you into believing it's much bigger than it really is—about the size of a mouse.

The warm sunshine brings out the aromas of the cedar and bay laurel trees. Around the grassy, sun-dappled meadows are great stands of oaks, maples, and firs and pines standing two hundred feet tall and more. And all around are the gray granite walls and peaks and domes towering almost a mile above the valley floor.

There was a time not too long ago when few people knew this place. But there was one who came here to live and spend much of his life among the waterfalls, the summer flowers, and the deep snows of winter. Had you come here then, you might have caught a glimpse of him. You might have seen him sitting in a meadow, sketching flowers and recording their names in his notebook. Or maybe you'd have seen this lone figure climbing hand over hand up a steep rock face to get closer to a waterfall. You'd have recognized him if you saw him.

He's tall, thin, "a farmer-looking man," a friend once said. He has curly hair; a full, long brown beard; and keen gray eyes. When he climbs over rocks and boulders, he almost dances from one to the other.

He wears an old, battered slouch hat and strides briskly along a narrow trail or sits looking outward atop one of the great peaks. To the people he meets, he introduces himself as John Muir. And he tells them all about the animals, the birds, the plants, the trees and rocks of Yosemite.

He's young, yet he's been so many places, seen so much. He's wandered up into Canada. He's walked from Indiana to the Gulf of Mexico "holding a generally southward course," as he puts it, "like the birds when they are going from summer to winter."

He's even sailed from the Gulf of Mexico to San Francisco, rounding the tip of South America along the way. But, as we shall see, this was not unusual behavior for the Scotsman who "loved to wander."

△△△

Johnny Muir grew up in the Scottish countryside that gave his family their name. *Muir* means "moor"—rolling, open wasteland covered with brush and heather. "Fortunately around my native town of Dunbar, by the North Sea," John tells us, "there was no lack of wildness. . . . I loved to wander in the fields to hear the birds sing, and along the sea-shore to gaze and wonder at the shells and sea-weeds, eels and crabs in the pools among the rocks when the tide was low; and best of all to watch the waves in awful storms thundering on the black headlands."

As a young boy, John explored the outdoors. He and his friends climbed into the trees in search of birds' nests and counted the beautiful eggs inside. Later, they climbed into the trees again to watch the little fledglings being fed and, later, learning to fly. The children were learning, in their own way, much about the natural world around them.

Johnny went to school only a few years in Scotland. But they were hard years. "We had to get three lessons every day in Latin, three in

French, and as many in English, besides spelling, history, arithmetic and geography. In addition to all this, father made me learn so many Bible verses every day that by the time I was eleven years of age I had about three fourths of the Old Testament and all of the New by heart."

Johnny didn't much like his school and looked forward to reaching, as he put it, "the wonderful, school-less, book-less, American wilderness."

In 1849, when John was just 11, his family moved to a farm in Wisconsin. Wisconsin was the newest state in the Union, barely a year old. Much of the land was wild forests and open, rumpled plains. And there were lakes, thousands of them, everywhere you looked.

Soon young John came to know the names of Wisconsin's flowers and trees, its birds and animals and insects, as well as he knew his Bible verses. He thought of these and all living creatures as friends. Later, when his two daughters, Wanda and Helen, were growing up, he taught them the names of the plants and birds in the garden. "For how would you like it," he asked them, "if people didn't call you by your name?"

That's what was so special about John Muir. He didn't think of himself as separate from the natural world as many people did then. He felt always part of it. "Most people are *on* the world not in it," he said once regretfully, "alone like marbles of polished stone, touching but separate."

△ △ △

In the early 1860s, John Muir left the family farm and attended the University of Wisconsin. Abraham Lincoln was President then, and the nation was torn apart by the Civil War. After the war, John left college and began the long journey that took him on foot to the Gulf of Mexico and then by boat to San Francisco.

But John didn't like cities. So he didn't stay long in them. "I stopped one day in San Francisco and then inquired for the nearest way out of town. 'But where do you want to go?' asked

the man. . . . 'To any place that is wild,' I said."
John was directed to the ferry that took him to
Oakland.

Soon he was in wild, open country again.
He carried his usual gear—a small bag with a
change of clothes, his notebook, a hair brush,
and pieces of bread. When he had walked about
forty miles inland, he reached a mountain pass
where he could look out on the broad, flat San
Joaquin Valley for the first time.

It was, he recalled, "level like a lake of
gold—floweriest part of the world" he had ever
seen. And there in the distance, gleaming white
against the blue sky, was the Sierra Nevada, the
"Snowy Range." And in that distance was
the wild mountain land his heart longed for.
"So on the first of April, 1868, I set out afoot for
Yosemite."

John walked toward the mountains and,
many days later, found himself among them. He
slept under the open sky. "How deep our sleep
last night in the mountain's heart, beneath the
trees and stars, hushed by solemn-sounding

waterfalls, and many small soothing voices in sweet accord whispering peace!"

The Sierra would be John Muir's home all his life to come. He liked to call it "The Range of Light" and wrote a poem by that name about his wilderness home.

And after ten years spent in the heart of it,
rejoicing and wondering, bathing in its glorious
    floods of light,
seeing the sunbursts of morning among the icy peaks,
the noonday radiance on the trees and rocks and snow,
the flush of alpenglow,
and a thousand dashing waterfalls with
    their marvelous abundance or irised spray,
it still seems to me above all others
    the range of light

2

Teddy's Museum

When John Muir was walking across America and making his way toward California, Theodore Roosevelt was just a little kid. Teddy lived in New York City, and John Muir's California was as far away as any place he could imagine.

Like Muir as a boy, Teddy dreamed of the wilderness, too, but he couldn't climb trees and rocks or go wandering the fields and seashore. Teddy was almost always sick. He suffered from asthma and poor eyesight and spent most of his early days indoors.

One day, in the family library, Teddy found a picture book about African animals that so enchanted him that he decided to learn all he could about nature.

As he got older, Teddy's health got better, which meant he could go outside. And he got glasses that helped him to see. So off he went in search of birds and all the little creatures he had been reading about during his long illness.

When he was seven years old, he began collecting specimens—plants, birds, insects, small animals. He learned to preserve the bodies of birds and to mount them in lifelike poses. He called his collection "The Roosevelt Museum of Natural History."

Teddy's Museum of Natural History included over two hundred birds he had collected and mounted himself. His was probably the biggest collection any boy his age had ever put together. Later, when he was a grown-up, he donated his specimens to the Smithsonian Institution in Washington, D.C.

When he was nine Teddy wrote a book about insects. "All the insects that I write about in this book," he noted, "inhabbit North America. Now and then a friend has told me something about them but mostly I have gained their habits from ofserv-a-tion."

Teddy didn't go to school as a child, but was tutored and self-taught. He did go to college—to Harvard—to study natural history. All his childhood he had wanted to be a naturalist when he grew up. As often happens, though, that plan changed. He became interested in politics and began studying for a career in law.

In the next few years, TR, as he became known, would have many important positions in government. He would become a police chief for New York City, an Assistant Secretary of the Navy, and later he would be elected Governor of New York. (And yes, he became a better speller.)

Important as he was, TR still found time to roam the wilderness, birding and hiking. Only now he was beginning to notice how the American wilderness had changed since he was a child. The prairie grasses were gone, grazed and trampled by too many cattle and sheep. Without the protective cover of the grasses, the land had eroded and turned to dust blowing in the wind.

The buffalo, elk, and wild sheep were gone. Grizzly bears, too, had been hunted almost to extinction. Beavers had been trapped for so long only a few had survived. The beaver dams, which had created so many of the little ponds Americans fished and swam in, lay abandoned and broken. Only hard, dry, cracked soil remained where once there was water filled with life.

Theodore Roosevelt began to feel personally responsible for what was happening. He had a large cattle ranch in the Dakota Territory. And he always enjoyed hunting. He began to realize how he had contributed to the changes in the wilderness.

True, he had always been a fair and responsible hunter. And his cattle herds were not as large as some. But he was one hunter and one rancher among hundreds of thousands of others. There were enough guns and livestock to change America—forever.

Now he rode his horse across sun-baked earth that had once been America's rich grasslands. Now there was only silence where once you could hear the thunder of great herds of buffalo. And he began to think of ways he might help.

△△△ 3 △△△
A Changing America

It wasn't just the wilderness that had changed since Theodore Roosevelt's childhood. Those years also brought a lot of changes to America's cities. More and more Americans were moving from the country to the cities. At the same time, millions of new immigrants were coming into American cities. The cities became crowded and their problems became worse.

As life in the cities became noisier, dirtier, and more crowded, the wilderness became more important. People went there to get away from the city. It was easy. In many cities it was just a short streetcar ride to a park or a little farther out to the forests, mountains, and open prairies. City children joined the Boy Scouts or Girl Scouts to learn wilderness and camping skills. Americans were beginning to value their wilderness. "They were," as John Muir wrote, "beginning to find out that going to the mountains is going home."

But America's wilderness home was in danger. John Muir knew that almost from the beginning of his travels. Our natural resources were not limitless as they seemed to the first settlers. In fact, they were fast disappearing. Millions of acres of trees had been cut for lumber without any thought of renewing the forests. In California, the old redwoods and even John's favorites, the sequoias, were threatened. Whole forests were being burned in the northwest to clear farmland and make pasture for sheep— "hooved locusts," John Muir called them.

It had always been this way here. Americans had used up millions of acres of farmland and then, because there was always more "out west," simply abandoned it. Americans had reached the Pacific Ocean and now there wasn't another frontier to move on to.

John Muir did not object to using the forests—it was the wasting and ruining of forests he wanted to stop. He wasn't against raising sheep either. Back when he first came to the Sierra, he worked as a shepherd and counted many sheep ranchers among his friends. But too many sheep grazing on too few acres had ruined too much land.

Neither did John want people kept out of the wilderness—all those city folks coming to the woods and mountains to get away were only doing what John had done. No, John wanted all Americans to be able to enjoy their wilderness. That was his point. He wanted to make sure there was a wilderness for everyone to enjoy.

He helped create a group called the Sierra Club, and with them he invited hundreds of people to Yosemite and took them for walks. He began writing books and articles for magazines warning Americans about what they had to lose if they didn't take care of their wilderness.

In his articles John called for the government to save and protect the most beautiful places by making them parks. "Through all the wonderful, eventful centuries since Christ's time—and long before that," he wrote, "God has cared for these trees . . . but he can not save them from fools—only Uncle Sam can do that."

In 1872, Congress had already created Yellowstone National Park as the first protected wilderness area in the United States. Congress then authorized three additional national parks in 1890: Yosemite, Sequoia, and General Grant.[1] John Muir felt this was barely a beginning. More national parks than these would be needed to save America's wilderness.

Nor was he happy that the new Yosemite National Park did not include his beloved Yosemite Valley. That, too, must be protected. But we must hurry, he warned. The lumbermen and sheepherders were already there. "The ground is already being gnawed and trampled into a desert," he wrote.

△ △ △

---

[1] now known as Kings Canyon National Park

△ 20 △

On September 14, 1901, Theodore Roosevelt had just hiked down off the highest mountain in the Adirondacks when he was told that President McKinley was dying. The President had been mortally wounded by an assassin's bullets. Less than a year earlier, Teddy Roosevelt had been elected Vice-President of the United States. At 42, he was about to become the youngest man ever to reach the presidency. When President McKinley died, a politician who hated TR groaned, "Now look! That damned cowboy is President of the United States."

TR had been a cowboy, had ridden herd on long cattle drives. He had written books about the American West and about his wilderness travels. He was also known and respected for his work as a naturalist. In fact, in 1897 a new species of mountain elk was named *Cervus roosevelti* in his honor. For someone who had spent his childhood creating his own museum and writing books about bugs, this must have been a dream come true!

Now, as President, he walked the White House grounds after breakfast listening to the birds. He recognized the song of new arrivals in the spring, and knew, too, when they had left. During his first year in office, he created new protected forests and wilderness areas. And in the quiet of the White House library, the President read the works of John Muir. He agreed with Muir and shared his love of the wilderness. The mountain man and the new President had lived in two very different worlds and so had never met. But TR would take care of that in short order.

The President planned a western trip for the spring of 1903. He sent word to John Muir that he wanted them to go tramping through the Sierra together, wanted John to show him the beautiful Yosemite Valley he had heard so much about but had never seen. "I do not want anyone with me but you," the President wrote John Muir, "and I want to drop politics absolutely for four days and just be out in the open with you."

John Muir didn't care much for "famous" people. The fact that the President of the United

States wanted to meet him didn't impress the naturalist either. As a matter of fact, he wasn't sure he wanted to meet the President. John and some friends were planning a trip to Europe and Asia in the spring. The President's visit would only get in the way of John's plans. True, the President had created a new Bureau of Forestry to regulate the use of the forests. But John cared little for Roosevelt's newly appointed head forester, Gifford Pinchot. Pinchot's interest in preserving forests was not, as he had said, "because they are beautiful or wild or the habitat of wild animals; [but] to ensure a steady supply of timber. . . ." You can imagine what John Muir thought about that!

In the end, John decided he would see the President. "I might be able to *do some forest good* in freely talking about the campfire."

△△△ 4 △△△

Roughing It

May 1903—glorious days in California's Yosemite Valley. Two men pose for the photographer at the very edge of a cliff four thousand feet above the valley floor.

In the background are snow-covered peaks of the Sierra Nevada mountains and Yosemite Falls, one of the highest in all the world. The raging water, icy from melting snow, leaps out over the edge of the valley, falling, falling, falling 2,425 feet to the rocks below. Yosemite Falls is ten times higher than the great Niagara.

Up here it is calm and quiet. Breezes whisper through the pines. The trees at this elevation are sparse, gnarled and bent by wind and deep snow. Some are centuries old and, yet, stand only three or four feet tall. A fluttering of wings and tiny mountain chickadees dart in and out of the trees foraging for seeds and insects.

The two men smile as they watch one of these little acrobats of the forest hang upside down from a small branch. *Chick-a-dee-dee, chick-a-dee-dee* is its call, and from far away comes the distant roar of the falls.

The man on the left is familiar to every American, with his mustache and round wire-rimmed glasses, the red bandanna tied around his neck, and the big Stetson cowboy hat. He wears a sweater and jacket—even in May, early morning temperatures are right around freezing up here—and his trousers are tucked into high leather boots. Actually, he's put on a clean, neat hat for this photograph. In his right hand he holds his favorite old hat, the one he has fun in. It's soft, beat-up, ragged around the edges, and shapeless. He'll put this one back on right after the photographer clicks the shutter. But for

now, it doesn't go with the pose or his high office. He is Theodore Roosevelt and he's the President of the United States.

The man with him, of course, is John Muir. John has lived in these Sierra mountains off and on for over thirty years. "When I was a boy in Scotland," John tells his new friend as they wait for the picture to be taken, "I was fond of everything that was wild, and all my life I've grown fonder of wild places and wild creatures."

So it was that the two finally met. And the photograph of the President and the now famous naturalist was taken high up on Glacier Point. John, too, was dressed up for the occasion . . . well, perhaps, a little bit neater than he usually was.

The President could not help liking this man who looked like he lived in the outdoors. By now John Muir was in his sixties, but still straight and tall as a redwood. His long, curly hair and scraggly beard were now as gray as his deep-set eyes. He, too, wore his favorite old scruffy hat.

They set off at once on horseback by themselves. A cook and two packers went on ahead with the camping gear and prepared the meals. And for three days the President and the naturalist roughed it and became dear friends.

The peaks of the Sierra Nevada were still white with snow. John showed all his favorite places to the President. They camped among a grove of giant sequoia trees. TR stared up in awe at the biggest sequoia John had found in the grove—325 feet tall and over thirty-five feet across at the base.

John told his friend the story of having found one of these trees burned half through by some great forest fire long ago. It took Muir a day to estimate the sequoia's age. First, he cleaned off the charred surface. Then, using his pocket lens, he counted each of the annual rings. "I counted over 4000 rings, which showed that this tree was in its prime, swaying in the Sierra winds, when Christ walked the earth. No other tree in the world, as far as I know, has looked down on so many centuries as the sequoia."

That night, John made his friend a bed of crisscrossed evergreen boughs. Then, as it got dark and cold, he built a big, heartwarming campfire.

They sat and talked through much of the night. The fire crackled. "It was clear weather," TR later recalled, "and we lay in the open." The towering cinnamon-colored trunks seemed to him like the columns of some grand and beautiful cathedral, grander than any human architect could ever dream of building.

The President had a lot of questions. He had come to see Yosemite, but more important, to talk to John. He asked the old man of the mountains what he knew about the destruction of the forests nearby. He wanted to know how badly overgrazing had eroded the soil. And he wanted suggestions about what might be done about it.

Well, TR had certainly come to the right place and the right man to ask these questions! John had an earful all ready for the President. Later, when they fell silent, TR heard a familiar bird song. "Did you hear that, John?" John hadn't. "It's a hermit thrush." TR couldn't see the little spotted brown thrush with its reddish tail, but he recognized its flutelike song.

TR was intrigued by his new friend. Their interests were different, but they could help each other. TR knew much about birds and animals, going back to his collecting and studying as a boy. But he didn't know much about geology and botany. The rocks, cliffs, mountains, and flowers and trees were what John knew best. So as they talked together, they learned from each other.

John threw another log onto the fire. The President slipped down into his bedroll and fell asleep to the wail of a mountain coyote somewhere distant in the night. "I was surprised," John wrote later, "to find he knew so much natural history."

The next day they were up early and rode hard through the forests and snowfields. Excited, the President pointed to a giant grizzly bear loping along on the next ridge.

They stopped, dismounted, and rested on the sun-warmed granite. Watching the grizzly watching them, TR told the story of the time he was charged by a grizzly.

The giant bear was on him, so close he could feel its hot breath. Instinctively, he raised his gun—he had time for but one shot—and fired. The bear fell dead almost at his feet.

"What a beautiful animal he was too," the President recalled, "probably weighed over a thousand pounds." The memory brought back his sadness at having to kill such a magnificent animal. "The older I grow the less I care to shoot anything except varmints," he said to John. "I am still something of a hunter, although lover of nature first."

TR was especially saddened by the growing number of animals becoming extinct, like the giant grizzly, disappearing from the American forests forever. "When I hear of the destruction of a species," he said, "I feel just as if all the works of some great writer had perished."

△△△ 5 △△△

Something Rare to Show Us

On they went that day. TR delighted in the sharp, high-pitched shriek of the marmots, sunning themselves at the doorways of their little caves in the broken-rock talus. As the horses came closer, the marmots galloped like little bears and disappeared to safety among the rocks.

On the south-facing slopes, the first wildflowers were blooming. Purple Shooting Stars and the tawny-yellow Golden Brodiaea carpeted the glistening wet soil between the rocks and snowfields. John mentioned to the President that American Indians dug up Brodiaea bulbs for food. A raucous chorus of treetoads came up from the warm edges of the lakes freed from winter ice. Their croaking echoed through the valley, *kreck-eck, kreck-eck, kr-r-r-eck.*

That night they camped high up on Glacier Point in a grove of fir trees overlooking Yosemite Valley below. Here they were at 7,214 feet looking down at a sheer rugged cliff falling from their feet to the valley floor more than 3,000 feet below. To the right, John said, they could see Half Dome, sliced in half by a glacier of ice almost a mile deep that carved out the valley. To the left, down the valley, they could see the massive granite face of El Capitan.

The President stood in silent awe at the scene that reached to the distant mountains and darkening sky. No sooner had they made camp and had their supper, when snow began to fall. At first, only a few large flakes drifted down through the trees, but then there were more flakes—and more—and soon the air was a flurry of white. John built a big campfire and

they talked again, each sharing what they knew about life and the wilderness.

John Muir and Theodore Roosevelt had so many stories to tell. John surely entertained the President with the story about the time he found himself in a violent windstorm. As he walked through the forest, trees splintered and crashed down all around him. But he wasn't afraid.

"I lost no time pushing out into the woods to enjoy it. For on such occasions Nature has always something rare to show us."

John found the tallest tree—about a hundred feet high—and climbed to its top. He hung on tightly as "the slender tops fairly flapped and swished . . . bending and swirling backward and forward, round and round."

The President must have laughed heartily at the image of John clinging to the tree-tops, swinging back and forth in a great arc, riding out the terrible storm like some hero in a tall tale.

That next morning John and the President awoke to find a four-inch blanket of snow on their bedrolls. They explored Glacier Point together, rode out to Nevada Fall, and, late in the afternoon, returned to the valley below.

Both men felt sadness at parting after being so close in the wilderness. John was taken with TR. "I had a glorious time with the President," he wrote to his daughters Wanda and Helen, "camped out alone with him 3 nights, in the Sequoia Grove, back of Glacier Point, & at foot of Yosemite near Bridal Veil." In another letter, John wrote, "I never before had so interesting, hearty, and manly a companion. I fairly fell in love with him."

After the days with John Muir, President Roosevelt saw more clearly what he must do. "We are not building this country of ours for a day," he reminded all Americans. "It is to last through the ages."

During his term as President, TR brought millions of acres of forest under government protection. Yosemite Valley was finally added to Yosemite National Park. He created 5 new national parks and 16 national monuments. No doubt recalling the joys of childhood, he also had set aside 51 wild bird refuges all over the country.

But, more important, the President did what he knew would please his friend John Muir the most. He made clear that greedy and wasteful destruction of the forests would no longer be allowed. Together, John Muir and Theodore Roosevelt had made the government responsible for protecting and preserving America's wilderness.

Afterword

Yosemite has always been a special place for me. I remember visiting the Valley for the first time almost thirty years ago. The thundering waterfalls and the mountains blanketed by snowy glaciers were magic to me.

I've returned to Yosemite many times since then, and each time I find something new that enchants me. Each time I go, I take along a favorite companion, John Muir, whose writings from long ago help me understand the water, the rocks, the trees, and the animals of the Valley.

I've retraced a few of John Muir's walks, although it would take almost a lifetime to walk where he walked. I've also told John Muir's stories to my friends and students so that they, too, may enjoy his Yosemite. That's why I've told you one of John Muir's favorite tales: about a camping trip in the Yosemite with the President of the United States, and the lifelong friendship that grew between the mountain man and the President.

In addition to visiting the places that John Muir described, I have also had the pleasure of reading works by both Muir and TR. Both men were good writers. Any quotes you see in the story come from works written by or about Muir and TR. They are their words as they were recorded in their time.

Notes

Page 2 A pika is a small mammal that looks like a rabbit, except for its short ears. It inhabits mountainous areas of Asia and western North America.

Page 6 Wisconsin entered the Union as the thirtieth state on May 29, 1848.

Page 7 The San Francisco that John Muir saw when he visited the city was one of contrasts. The silver extracted from the Comstock mines in the Nevada Territory provided money to erect bridges, pave roads, and construct hundreds of new buildings. However, downtown streets paved with wooden planks and storeowners' merchandise displayed on wooden sidewalks were still common sights.

Page 8 The Sierra Nevada run for about four hundred miles in eastern California. At places the mountain range is almost seventy miles wide. Its highest peak is Mt. Whitney. At 14,495 feet, Mt. Whitney is the highest peak in the United States outside Alaska.

Although the Sierra Nevada was a place of serene beauty, only a truly knowledgeable and hardy person, such as John Muir, could survive the area's rugged landscape and sometimes harsh weather. Even in April, temperatures regularly dipped below freezing, and sudden blizzards could still rage in the springtime.

Page 12 Today, the term "birding" means just observing a bird in its natural environment and classifying it. Back in Theodore Roosevelt's time, however, birding often involved shooting the bird under study. This was not considered unusual because back then people generally did not have powerful cameras or sighting instruments. Thus, to study a bird closely, it often was necessary to kill it.

Page 18 The Sierra Club is an organization devoted to protecting the environment. This protection includes saving threatened natural resources, scenic areas, and wildlife. The Club was founded in 1892 in San Francisco by John Muir, who became its first president. Now, having celebrated its hundredth birthday, the Sierra Club continues to work tirelessly on behalf of the environment.

Page 21 The highest peak in the Adirondack Mountains is Mount Marcy. At 5,344 feet high, Mount Marcy is also the tallest peak in New York State.

Page 28 The tree rings, or growth rings, that Muir observed can tell much about a tree's history. Each year a tree forms a new layer of wood just inside the bark. The number of these layers (rings) tells how long the tree has been living. The width of the rings also gives information about the climate during the year. A wide ring means that the growing season was good that year. A thin ring means that the growing season was poor that year.

David Weitzman is a writer and illustrator who lives in Point Reyes Station, California. His many books include *My Backyard History* and *Superpower: The Making of a Steam Locomotive.*